Native Americans

Choctaw

Barbara A. Gray-Kanatiiosh

ABDO Publishing Company

visit us at
www.abdopublishing.com

Cover Photo: Clyde H. Smith/Peter Arnold
Interior Photos: Corbis p. 30; Peter Arnold pp. 4, 29
Illustrations: David Kanietakeron Fadden pp. 7, 9, 11, 13, 15, 17, 19, 21, 23, 25, 27
Editors: Rochelle Baltzer, Heidi M. Dahmes
Art Direction & Maps: Neil Klinepier

Library of Congress Cataloging-in-Publication Data

Gray-Kanatiiosh, Barbara A., 1963-
  Choctaw / Barbara A. Gray-Kanatiiosh.
    p. cm. -- (Native Americans)
  Includes bibliographical references and index.
  ISBN-10 1-59197-653-7
  ISBN-13 978-1-59197-653-0
  1. Choctaw Indians--History--Juvenile literature. 2. Choctaw Indians--Social life and customs--Juvenile literature. [1. Choctaw Indians. 2. Indians of North America--Southern States.] I. Title. II. Series: Native Americans (Edina, Minn.)

E99.C8G73 2006
976.004'97387--dc22   2003070812

About the Author: Barbara A. Gray-Kanatiiosh, JD

Barbara Gray-Kanatiiosh, JD, Ph.D. ABD, is an Akwesasne Mohawk. She resides at the Mohawk Nation and is of the Wolf Clan. She has a Juris Doctorate from Arizona State University, where she was one of the first recipients of ASU's special certificate in Indian Law. Barbara's Ph.D. is in Justice Studies at ASU. She is currently working on her dissertation, which concerns the impacts of environmental injustice on indigenous culture. Barbara works hard to educate children about Native Americans through her writing and Web site, where children may ask questions and receive a written response about the Haudenosaunee culture. The Web site is: www.peace4turtleisland.org

About the Illustrator: David Kanietakeron Fadden

David Kanietakeron Fadden is a member of the Akwesasne Mohawk Wolf Clan. His work has appeared in publications such as *Akwesasne Notes*, *Indian Time*, and the *Northeast Indian Quarterly*. Examples of his work have also appeared in various publications of the Six Nations Indian Museum in Onchiota, NY. His work has also appeared in "How the West Was Lost: Always the Enemy," produced by Gannett Production, which appeared on the Discovery Channel. David's work has been exhibited in Albany, NY; the Lake Placid Center for the Arts; Centre Strathearn in Montreal, Quebec; North Country Community College in Saranac Lake, NY; Paul Smith's College in Paul Smiths, NY; and at the Unison Arts & Learning Center in New Paltz, NY.

Contents

Where They Lived

The Choctaw (CHAHK-taw) **dialect** is from the Muskogean language family. When President Andrew Jackson spoke with the Choctaw, he imitated the phrase *hoka hay*. This Choctaw expression was used to communicate agreement. Eventually, the phrase became the word "okay."

Choctaw homelands were located in the Southeast. Choctaw territory included parts of present-day Mississippi, Alabama, and Louisiana. The Mississippi River formed the area's western boundary. Neighboring tribes included the Chickasaw, Natchez, Caddo, and Creek.

Various features were found on Choctaw homelands. Some areas were covered with hilly grasslands. Other parts were filled with forests of oak, hickory, and pine trees.

Swamplands were commonly found on Choctaw territory.

4

Bald cypress trees and sweet gum trees grew in the swamplands. And, Spanish moss often hung from the trees.

Many animals lived on Choctaw territory. Alligators and turtles roamed along the rivers and in the swamplands. Frogs and snakes also made their homes in these areas.

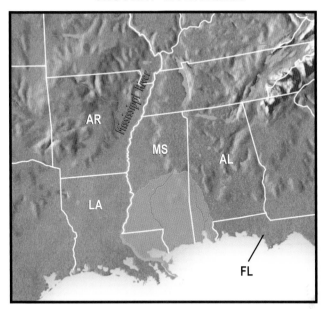

Choctaw Homelands

5

Society

Choctaw society was split into two *iksas*, or parts. Children belonged to their mother's iksa. A person was forbidden to marry someone in his or her own iksa.

The Choctaw lived in villages. Each village had a chief to represent and protect the people. Chiefs met with a council of elders to discuss the needs of the village. And, they conducted ceremonies. Each chief had an assistant to help organize festivals and announce messages.

District chiefs were another group of Choctaw leaders. They were responsible for a particular area of villages. District chiefs met individually with the village chiefs in their area to discuss issues. When a very important matter arose, all of the district chiefs met with all of the village chiefs. Together, they came to a conclusion.

Each village also had a war chief. These leaders trained young warriors to protect the villages. Each war chief had two assistants to help carry out his orders.

District chiefs often discussed matters with other community leaders.

7

Food

The Choctaw gathered, hunted, and fished. They were also advanced gardeners. The rivers on Choctaw land often flooded, which created fertile farmland. So, they usually had excess produce to trade.

The men prepared the land for planting. To do this they burned brush, and they cut down trees with stone axes. Then, the women planted and tended the gardens. They used bone hoes to weed and till the soil.

Corn was an important crop for the Choctaw. It was the foundation for many recipes, and it was dried for winter use. Besides corn, the Choctaw planted beans, squashes, melons, pumpkins, and sunflowers.

The women gathered wild fruits, vegetables, nuts, and herbs. They also collected tree bark, roots, and wild plants. They used these to add flavor to food and to make medicine and drinks.

The men hunted deer, bears, geese, rabbits, turkeys, and ducks with bows and arrows. To catch smaller animals, they used traps, blowguns, and rabbit sticks.

Fishing was common among Choctaw men. They often caught trout and shrimp. Sometimes, they captured alligators in the swamps. They fished with bows and arrows, spears, nets, and hooks and lines. Fish and other meats were dried in the sun or smoked over a fire for later use.

The Choctaw used cane to build blowguns. And, they carved wood to make the darts. Then, they attached cotton or thistle to one end of the dart to help it fly straight.

9

Homes

   The Choctaw lived in rectangular-shaped homes with triangular roofs. They used materials found in nature to build their homes. Constructing a home was a step-by-step process.

   To build the frame, the Choctaw used wooden poles. First, they buried the poles in the ground. Then, they tied crossbeams to the poles using rope made from bark or plant fibers. To form the walls, they wove branches and vines into the frame. Then, they tied woven mats onto the walls.

   Finally, the Choctaw covered the outside of the home with **daub**. This protected the interior from harsh weather. They left an opening in the side of the home for a door. And, they left a hole in each end of the roof for smoke to escape.

   Inside the homes, there were beds made from branches. The Choctaw covered the beds with woven mats, hides, or fur robes. They made another kind of blanket from turkey feathers. First, they twisted the feathers and rolled them into a string. Then, they wove the string to make a blanket.

The Choctaw used natural materials to build their homes. The roofs were made from thatch.

Clothing

The Choctaw wore clothing made from deer hides. The women were in charge of making the clothing. First, they scraped away the meat and hairs from the hides. Then, they **tanned** the hides to make them soft. Next, they stretched them on a frame to dry.

When the hides were dry, the women sewed them together to make clothing. They used needles and **awls** carved from bone and thread made from deer **sinew** or plant fibers.

The women wore dresses. And, they wore decorated combs in their hair. The men wore **breechcloths** and shirts, as well as woven sashes. The sashes were hung over the shoulder and tied at the waist. Both men and women wore moccasins on their feet. The moccasins had a single front seam with ankle flaps.

Choctaw clothing styles changed after they began trading with the Europeans. The Choctaw traded animal hides and furs for cloth, beads, ribbons, premade clothing, and silver. They used the silver to make combs, armbands, and special oval-shaped necklaces called *gorgets*. Choctaw men began wearing low-crowned black felt hats. And, women started decorating their clothing with ribbons.

Before they received European goods, the Choctaw wore clothing made from hides and plant materials.

Crafts

Choctaw women often wove baskets. They used cane to weave the baskets and vegetable dyes to color them. The Choctaw used the baskets for carrying and storing things. The women also used cane to weave mats for sitting or sleeping on. Sometimes, they hung them on the wall for decoration.

Choctaw men built the equipment that was needed for games, such as stickball. They carved stickball rackets from hickory wood. The rackets were about 30 inches (76 cm) long. The men carved one end of the racket to form a loop. Then, they wove the looped end with **sinew** to make a net. To make the ball, the men wrapped a stone in animal hide and covered it with woven sinew.

The men also made their hunting tools. They carved rabbit sticks from wood. These were about 18 inches (46 cm) long and shaped like a boomerang. One end had a handle, and the other end was curved. Men used rabbit sticks to kill small animals.

To fish, men used hooks made from bone. To make these, they cut hollow bird bones into sections. Then, they carved the bones into hooks.

Men were in charge of making the equipment for games, such as stickball.

15

Family

The Choctaw lived with their **extended families**. Families attended ceremonies and festivals together. **Rituals** took place at certain ceremonies. The most important religious ceremony for the Choctaw was the Green Corn Festival. This was held during the summer to celebrate the ripening of corn. It was also a time of forgiveness and purification.

To prepare, the Choctaw cleaned their homes and village buildings. They also **fasted** for two days. Near the end of the festival, a high priest lit a fire. This represented the start of a new year. Then, the priest led the elders in a dance around the fire.

At some festivals, the Choctaw played games. Stickball was a favorite game among them. Named "la crosse" by the French, this game was often played between Choctaw villages to establish peace. Spiritual leaders attended stickball games. Their prayers and powers were thought to affect the game's outcome.

The object of stickball was to use two netted rackets to launch a ball to the opponent's goal. Players were not allowed to use their hands. Instead, they used the rackets to pick up, pass, catch, and throw the ball.

Stickball games could involve as few as 20 players, or as many as 300 players.

Children

A flat forehead on a Choctaw man was a sign of beauty. To obtain this look, the Choctaw used a device that applied pressure to a male infant's forehead. So, the Spanish explorers referred to the tribe as *chato*, which means "flat" in Spanish. Some people believe this is how the Choctaw got their name.

Elders taught Choctaw children about history and **culture**. Young boys and girls learned everyday tasks by helping with daily chores. They planted and weeded the gardens. And, they helped the women gather food.

The children were taught to respect nature. They learned to identify plants and animals and to live in harmony with them. When they had to kill animals or plants, they thanked them for giving up their lives.

Choctaw women taught the girls how to cook food, care for the younger children, prepare hides, and make clothing. Girls also made clothing for their dolls. This was good practice for making clothing for their families when they got older.

Choctaw men taught the boys how to make and use blowguns. A full-sized blowgun was up to seven feet (2 m) long, but boys used shorter ones. The boys also learned how to make other tools and weapons.

Village elders often told stories to help Choctaw children learn the tribe's history.

19

Myths

The Choctaw share many stories that have been passed on from older generations. These myths teach them about life. The following is a **migration** story. It explains how the Choctaw found their homelands.

A long time ago, a group of people lived in the Northwest. The land became too populated, and food was scarce. So two brothers, Chahta and Chicksa, led a migration.

The brothers asked the Great Spirit for help. So, the Great Spirit gave them a special pole. The pole was meant to guide them to their new home in a sacred, plentiful land.

To start, Chahta placed the pole in the ground. The next day it was leaning. So that day, the people traveled in the direction it leaned. This went on for days until they came to a river.

When they reached the river, Chahta placed the pole in the ground as usual. That night rain poured down on them, and the river flooded. The next morning, they found that the flooded river had separated the two leaders.

Chicksa continued northward, and his group became known as the Chickasaw. Chahta saw that the pole was standing straight, so his group stayed there. They became known as the Choctaw.

According to this migration myth, the flooded river separated the Choctaw from the Chickasaw.

War

Establishing peace was important to the Choctaw. They often met with neighboring tribes and discussed issues to prevent a war. Leaders sat on woven mats and passed around a calumet, or peace pipe. Pipe smoking was a sacred act. It helped to bring balance to the people.

But sometimes, the Choctaw could not establish a peaceful agreement. So, they fought to protect their people and lands. They were skilled warriors, and the women often went into battle with their husbands.

To prepare for war, each village held a dance. Most tribes did not allow women to take part in the war dances. But during one dance, Choctaw women joined the men. A victory during battle was also cause for a lively celebration. The entire village danced, and the warriors shared their stories.

Weapons of war were mostly the same as hunting tools. The Choctaw used bows and arrows and spears while in battle. During close combat, they used knives and **hatchets**.

Early weapons were made of stones, bones, horns, shells, antlers, or wood. After the Choctaw began trading with the Europeans, weaponry changed. The Choctaw began to use goods that they received during trades, such as guns and metal axes and arrowheads.

The Choctaw discussed disagreements with neighboring tribes to avoid fighting.

Contact with Europeans

The Spanish were the first Europeans to meet the Choctaw. Explorer Hernando de Soto and his group arrived in Choctaw territory around 1540. However, the meeting was not very friendly.

De Soto captured a Choctaw chief and demanded that the Choctaw carry his group's supplies. In return, de Soto would release the chief. The Choctaw were angry, so they made a plan.

The Choctaw tricked de Soto and his group into traveling to the next village. When they arrived at the village, the Choctaw held a feast and a dance. When de Soto was off guard, the Choctaw attacked him and his group. De Soto was injured, but the fight was not over. Before leaving, he burned several Choctaw villages and stole their corn.

By the early 1700s, the Choctaw had established good trade relations with the Europeans. At first, the Choctaw and the Europeans had difficulties because they spoke different languages. So, they developed a special trade language. They also used sign language to communicate with each other.

The French built trading posts along the Mississippi River. The Choctaw liked to trade with them. They had valuable goods such as guns, ribbons, felt hats, and glass beads. Eventually, the Choctaw formed an **alliance** with the French.

The Choctaw and the French developed special ways of communicating.

25

Pushmataha

Pushmataha (push-muh-TAH-hah) was born in Mississippi around 1765. He was a well-known Choctaw warrior, speaker, and negotiator. At a young age, Pushmataha established himself as a good warrior. He fought in battles against the Creek, Osage, and Caddo.

In 1805, Pushmataha became a tribal chief. During the Creek War of 1813–1814, he fought against the Creek and British. He also led 500 Choctaw men alongside General Andrew Jackson. For his services, Pushmataha received the rank of brigadier general in the U.S. Army.

Pushmataha embraced the ways of the new settlers more than other Choctaw leaders. He signed treaties that gave parts of Choctaw lands to them. But, he also promoted Native American rights.

In 1824, Pushmataha went to Washington, D.C., to strengthen relations between the Choctaw and the federal government. He hoped to use his speaking skills to protect the Choctaw.

But during the trip, Pushmataha was exposed to harsh weather. He became severely sick and died on December 24, 1824. Pushmataha was given a full military burial. He was buried in the Congressional Cemetery in Washington, D.C.

Pushmataha was a respected Choctaw leader.

The Choctaw Today

In 1830, the United States established the Indian Removal Act. This act was intended to move many Native American tribes from their homelands to make room for new settlers. The Choctaw were the first to be relocated. They were moved to present-day Oklahoma.

This forced relocation of Native American tribes is known as the Trail of Tears. Those on the trail were exposed to harsh weather. And there were shortages of food, blankets, horses, and wagons. About 2,500 Choctaw people died while on the journey.

Almost a century later, the Choctaw came to America's aid during the final days of World War I. A group called the Choctaw Code Talkers helped America defeat its enemies. The group sent messages in the Choctaw language that the enemies were unable to decode.

Choctaw was the first Native American language used for this purpose. The Choctaw offered this aid again during World War II. Today a memorial in Durant, Oklahoma, honors the World War I Choctaw Code Talkers.

The Choctaw Nation of Oklahoma and the Mississippi Band of Choctaw Indians are both **federally recognized**. Both groups live on **reservations** and have an elected government. The 2000 Census reported that 158,774 people claimed Choctaw ancestry.

Choctaw children are the next generation to maintain tribal traditions. So, learning about Choctaw culture is important. This Mississippi Choctaw girl is dressed in traditional clothing.

The Choctaw continue to make efforts to protect their **culture**. They teach classes to maintain Choctaw language and traditions. The Choctaw Nation of Oklahoma hosts a yearly Labor Day Festival. And, the Mississippi Band of Choctaw Indians hosts an annual Indian Fair. During these celebrations the Choctaw feast, dance, sing, and play stickball.

These Choctaw men are performing tribal dances in traditional clothing for tourists in Phoenix, Arizona. To the left, a man wears clothing covered in fringes. Below, a man wears a large feather headdress.

Glossary

alliance - people, groups, or nations joined for a common cause.

awl - a pointed tool for making small holes in materials such as leather or wood.

breechcloth - a piece of hide or cloth, usually worn by men, that wraps between the legs and ties with a belt around the waist.

culture - the customs, arts, and tools of a nation or people at a certain time.

daub - a mixture of sand, mud, clay, or crushed seashells used for construction.

dialect - a form of a language spoken in a certain area or by certain people.

extended family - a family that includes grandparents, uncles, aunts, and cousins in addition to a mother, father, and children.

fast - to go without food.

federal recognition - the U.S. government's recognition of a tribe as being an independent nation. The tribe is then eligible for special funding and for protection of its reservation lands.

hatchet - a short-handled ax often with a hammerhead to be used with one hand.

migrate - to move from one place to another, often to find food.

reservation - a piece of land set aside by the government for Native Americans to live on.

ritual - a form or order to a ceremony.

sinew - a band of tough fibers that joins a muscle to a bone.

tan - to make a hide into leather by soaking it in a special liquid.

Web Sites

To learn more about the Choctaw, visit ABDO Publishing Company on the World Wide Web at **www.abdopub.com**. Web sites about the Choctaw are featured on our Book Links page. These links are routinely monitored and updated to provide the most current information available.

Index